Choose Love

Edited by Lindsey Westwood
Photo by Natalie Minh
natalieminh.com

Second edition hardback

This book is dedicated to everyone who comes to a crossroad with a choice to make...I pray you Choose Love.

Contents

Desperate for a Loved One?

A Most Beautiful Ending

Dear Friend,

This little booklet/devotion was written out of questions that have been asked of me by people all over the country as I travel with my husband, as well as my own challenging and at times painful journey of faith and hope that I learned to trust in. I pray you find peace and God's grace for yourself and those around you who are hurting and need to feel His unfailing love.

In His Love,
Eileen Marx

God in Our Darkness

Even when the darkness is all around you... God from Heaven can see you and wants to rescue you from your darkest pain. He hurts for you; His love for you is so deep, so readily available to show you. He won't intrude. He won't push His way into your pain. He simply wants you to ask.

God wants you to come to Him in your pain... Cry out to Him; let Him know you need Him to heal your broken heart. He is ever waiting for you to cry out to Him, He longs to hear your voice, your fears, your doubt, and all that breaks your heart.

I remember seeing my husband, (7th degree black belt, Former Marine who is 6'2~ 200 lbs., able to kill someone in a matter of seconds), completely terrorized and crying out in pain and filled with so much fear as he was having a flash back of someone from his childhood who was hurting him. It was more than he could handle and was taking over his mind as though it was happening right then! He ran into the hot shower and dropped down to the floor with his knees to his chest and yelled out "Please don't let them kill me! Please don't let them kill me!"

In one of his darkest moments, completely out of his control, God showed up on his behalf. All I could see with my natural eyes was my husband running like a frightened child who was being chased as terror filled his heart… This is when something supernatural happened! God, a loving Father, did something on his behalf. My heart hurt for him so deeply; I didn't know what to do. I walked into the shower fully clothed and knelt down next to my husband and just held him. I didn't say a word, just cried with him and let him know that everything was going to be ok. Later my husband said, "I felt like God Almighty stepped into my pain and was holding me and letting me know how much He loved me."

I love that God was so personal to Victor to show him how much He loved him and truly met him in his darkest pain.

Have you ever felt like Victor did? Do you know that God Almighty wants to hold you and let you know just how much He loves you? God truly cares about your pain and broken heart. In fact there is a scripture that says, "*Jesus came to heal the broken hearted.*" –Isaiah 61:1

Would you allow God to heal you and your

broken heart? He is just a cry out away
from you.

Confusion & Darkness Live Together

How can a loving God cause such horrible things to happen to a child, an innocent child? God (a loving Father) is not the one that causes bad things to happen. He gives everyone a free will and people choose to do bad by their own choice.

This is where the confusion comes in. The One you need the most, the One who is able to heal you, you stay away from. You have believed (those voices in your head), that He was the one who caused the bad things to happen to you. All the while, He's been waiting for you to come to Him to find healing and freedom from so much pain, anger and bitterness. So much anger has been misdirected at the One who loves you the most.

There has been so much time lost in your life trying to get even and run from your past. There is a history of broken relationships in your past that you are questioning "Why? Why do I keep ruining relationships? Why can't I keep a job? Why do people keep using me and taking advantage of me?" You have tried to outrun your pain and memories only to find yourself still hurting and now years, maybe decades later it's the same pain, same anger, same resentment, and a ton of bitterness.

Confusion causes fear that keeps you from being able to face your past. It tells you, "Don't go there, don't tell anyone, and don't go to God. He knew all that happened and He just watched it happen. He didn't get you out of it. How can He even say He loves you?" Truth is, God does know about your past; He knows the pain you suffer today because of it. He knows about it, but He didn't cause it; He's not the one who inflicted evil on you. Just as the wrong things you have done towards others, God didn't stop you. He knew you were doing it and knows of the pain you have caused other people.

When we truly understand that each person has been given a free will to do good or evil towards another person, the idea that God has caused it or is to blame doesn't make sense anymore.

My father lived with bitterness towards his older brother because he was always bullying him and physically abusive towards him when they were children. At family gatherings, as grown men, he and his brother would fist fight as their wives and children watched. My dad held on to this childhood pain until well into his 60's. I'm not sure he was ever able to let go and find forgiveness for his brother. My dad was a very intelligent man with so many gifts and was used beautifully (the second part of his life) in so many people's lives. He helped thousands of people get clean and sober and free from substance abuse. He even founded a nationally recognized institute to help educate and train others to council people with addictions. The sad thing is, his first 20 years as a husband and father, as much as he hated being bullied, he ended up being a bully! It's so true what Hebrews 12:15 says about not letting a root of bitterness spring up causing trouble as it defiles many!

If you humble yourself and admit that you are hurting and allow God to go with you to that painful place, God will walk with you to those painful places and bring healing. He will bring truth about what happened and will show you more if you are willing to listen and accept more information, even those things that are so hard to accept.

How do you do that? You have to let it go. You have to get it out of your soul, speak it out, maybe even write it down telling God everything; He already knows. Ask Him to help you, free you from all those deadly emotions.

Next, ask Him to heal you and forgive you from the unforgiveness and bitterness you've kept deep in your soul infecting your heart. Ask Him to take you out of this darkness and pit of confusion and bring you into His marvelous light.

God takes it seriously when we hold on to grudges and do not forgive those who have wronged us. In fact, He says in Matthew 6:15 *"If you do not forgive men of their trespasses* (wrongs), *neither will your father forgive you for your trespasses."*

Mourning into Joy

Accepting & mourning what has happened to you is probably the hardest thing for you to allow yourself to do, but quite possibly the most freeing release of all the harmful emotions you have lived with.

Coming to terms and accepting that you didn't have the childhood or upbringing that you had dreamed of is like mourning the loss of a dream you know will never have happen. It's painful, frustrating and absolutely not fair! It's not fair. It's ok to grieve this and then acknowledge your disappointment, anger, and sadness.

When you're done saying **everything** you need to say, bring it to God and let Him take it from your heart and take care of it for you. He is able to carry our burdens and hurts so much more than you can.

As hard and strange as this may sound, start singing to Him and thanking Him for freeing you and taking this heavy weight you've been carrying. Start thanking Him for the life you have today, not about perfection, but the freedom and the ability your heart will have to see others pain, and the compassion that your heart will be able to feel and relate to other hurting souls. There are people who need to hear your story and hear how you overcame your deepest pain, bitterness & sorrows. You were created for more, much more than just pain and sadness...you have a future waiting for you.

"For I know the plans I have for you, says the Lord...to give you a future and a hope."
–Jeremiah 29:11

A Life-Changing Question

Wounded people hurt people, much of the time it's people closest to them. They don't want to repeat the vicious cycle, but they are stuck; they can't find a way out of their pain. By default they hurt and damage innocent people.

When you can ask this simple question, "I wonder what happened to them to make them so mean, angry, cold, hard?" it can change the way you feel about them enough to help you forgive them. Not excuse them, but forgive them...

When I was 20 years old I wrote my father a letter stating I was tired of acting like I enjoyed spending time with him and seeing my other siblings acting like they actually liked him.

We were all raised in fear of him as a verbally and physically abusive father and husband, all of which was never acknowledged and we all continued to gather at birthdays and holidays and pretended that everything was great!
To my surprise I received a letter from my dad (a former Marine and Korean War Vet). He acknowledged my feelings and then shared his fear of being a father, and really not knowing how to be a father. He said he felt insecure and acknowledged my mom as the one who really took most of the responsibility of raising us 8 kids. Wow! I never knew how he felt.

When I read his letter, it brought my heart so much compassion for my dad that I was able to forgive him for his abusive parenting. I still had to work through my anger towards him, but this helped me understand him better. What a different perspective it was to have more information. It truly changed my heart towards him.

A high school principal in Oregon changed the way he disciplined these hard kids who had severe attitude problems and were brought to him before the next step of discipline, which was expulsion from school. Instead of his normal routine of dishing out the handbook discipline, he started asking these troubled kids about how things were going at home. When these kids knew that this man cared about them and what was happening in their world at home, they started responding positively. He also started hugging these hurting teens. He could see that a simple hug was something that they needed more than a stern look or verbal reprimand.

When people are heard and know that how they feel matters and are validated, it really can change their behavior.

Is there someone in your life that you think about as you read this? Have you ever asked them about their past, maybe their childhood, or someone that has hurt them? I bet if you took the time to ask them, you may find out some things that you never knew or even considered. People don't outgrow pain they just get older and harder.

Peace for Despair

Anxiety, fear, and panic attacks are all symptoms of PTSD.

Your mind is remembering something that you're trying to fight and forget. Feelings of being overwhelmed with fear, terror, and anxiety has to be some of the worst emotions a human heart can experience. This is happening for a reason; something has triggered this reaction.

Do yourself a favor and ask God " What is going on?" Ask Him to show you and if you know what it is, ask Him to give you courage to face it with Him right there with you. Ask Him to peel back what you cannot see and bring it to the light, and walk with you through the darkness.

King David said, "Yea, though I walk through the valley of the shadow of death, I will fear no evil, for you are with me." – Psalm 23

He acknowledged that God was with him. God wants to give you peace, His peace instead of despair. If you believe in your heart that He is with you, you can have His peace in your mind. His peace can crush all fear and wipe out anxiety. The fear needs to be recognized and brought out to the light so it can be dealt with. Don't keep those thoughts to yourself, as they will only be magnified in your mind.

"You will keep him in perfect peace, whose mind is stayed on You, because he trusts You." –Isaiah 23:6

Jesus experienced such deep emotional

pain that He bled drops of blood as He was praying to His Father before He was crucified. He knew that the next several hours would be excruciating and more than He could bear. He understood fear, anxiety, loneliness and rejection, all these terrorizing human emotions. How could He not understand?

My daughter would routinely come into our room at night with paralyzing thoughts that she was going to die. She would say, "I'm know I'm going to die." She was being tormented by these horrible thoughts almost nightly. Even in her teenage years she would have these overwhelming thoughts. We would remind her that God is the one who knows when each of us is going to go be with Him. She eventually learned to trust God with each day and not to trust her feelings. She would read scriptures that promised hope and peace. She also realized these thoughts were just thoughts, not truth!

Because of her many nights of terror and feeling like she was going die, and didn't, she has so much compassion for those who suffer with anxiety. She understands how those feelings can make a soul fall into despair. She has learned to pray and overcome those terrifying thoughts.

The truth is, we all are going to die, but only when God is ready for us, not a moment before! God doesn't want us thinking about death; He conquered death at the cross. He wants us to live in the here and now, and look forward to spending eternity with Him.

More than You Know

Even before you were born, even before
your mom knew she was pregnant with you,
your life has been valued and counted,
every number of days that you will be here.
Every hair on your head is numbered.

I love my children fiercely and deeply, but I
couldn't imagine taking time to count every
hair on their head. Even if I did have the
time, I couldn't. But the One who created
you thinks it's pretty important to tell you
just how much he cares about you.

Do you know that every tear you have
shed is kept? (Read Psalm 56:8) Each tear
represents the tears of many different
events in your life and each one has been
noticed. Every time you sat and wept and
had tears roll down your face and you

thought nobody cared or cares for you, Jesus took notice.

You are valued even if you are not "good enough," "smart enough," have lots of money, a nice home, a nice car, clothes, jewelry, and a career. These things have little value in the light of eternity. Jesus didn't have even a bed to call His own.

Your worth is based on how God sees you, not how people see you. You won't have a closet in heaven to hold all of your nice clothes, a parking stall for that beautiful car, a deposit box for your jewelry, a key for your house or a mirror to see your hairdo. You have gifts, abilities, and talents that only you have. You are unique, one of a kind; no one else has your heart, mind, or even fingerprints! You are one of a kind! When negative thoughts come into your mind, don't own those, don't make them yours, and don't take it personal.

I remember driving one day, pulling up to a light, my mind was going to a place of feeling insecure about who I was and what I was doing... all of a sudden I heard this in my head, "You were created for My Glory, not man's." I just sat at that light and wept as I understood very clearly who was saying that to me.

When you start hearing those thoughts such as, "You don't measure up, you don't matter, how could you ever do something of worth?" or "you were a mistake!" stop, don't repeat those thoughts in your head. Speak the truth about who you are, as God is the One who created you, and He thinks you are of great value and worth!

A woman in her fifties came up to us after a service, well put together, beautiful lady, sharp clothes, nice car and all. After talking and praying with her, she realized her deepest fear was that she wasn't loved! She gasped when she realized that she had believed that she was not loved. It was a lie in her mind, not truth, but a lie that made her believe that.

Take every thought captive; bring it to Jesus and see what He has to say about it.

Forgive!

"Has anyone ever done anything to you to hurt you? Have you ever done something to hurt somebody else?" These are questions we ask these young kids that are locked up in youth facilities all over the country. They are locked up due to various crimes, but one of the common threads of what gets them locked up is anger and unforgiveness! They are holding grudges against someone who has wronged them. For these kids it usually is a parent, caregiver or the "system" who has abused, neglected or rejected them. We can't blame them for feeling the way they do, it's a normal response, but we do explain that if they don't forgive those who have hurt them, chances are they will repeat doing those things that got them locked up in the first place. They can pretend to be okay and even say it doesn't affect them. They may be able to move forward and do the steps to get out, but it will catch up to them.

The percentage rate of these kids coming back is astonishing. Yes, they work through the steps to get out and work on all the "outward" behavior, but sadly they don't deal with the root, and because of that, they begin repeating a vicious cycle. Their hearts can lie and hide, but their soul doesn't lie, and it speaks loudly!
Those closest to them are the ones who are hurt and often abused, because of this pain.

When a human heart is able to fully see just how much they have been forgiven for all the past, present and future sins, (not because they have earned it or that it is due them, but just simply receive it), when this happens they can see Jesus dying on the cross for their sins. Every one of them has been forgiven... When a heart is forgiven, washed and cleansed, it is then able to forgive those who have hurt, wronged and betrayed them.

It doesn't take a special recipe or ritual to receive this forgiveness, it simply takes a little bit of faith to believe that Jesus died on the cross for your sins. He willingly died a shameful death instead of you and me! The price to receive this forgiveness is free, however, it cost Jesus His life! Choose forgiveness... Don't waste another day, week, or year rehearsing bad things done to you. You were created with the ability to move on, to live an abundant life. God wants us to live an abundant life, not necessarily an easy one.

Amazing Love

If you find yourselves living with a loved one who has suffered with any type of trauma whether it's childhood trauma, other physical or verbal abuse or a returned Veteran, as difficult as this may sound, you can take this as a gift from God to help you demonstrate His love through you! There will be times when you have amazing opportunities to show God's unconditional love for your loved one, His long suffering, His patience, His gentleness, kindness and goodness. This won't happen in your own strength; you personally will run out of patience and longsuffering. You will have to be full of God's love, His amazing love.

Knowing how much God loves you, that He gave His only Son for you to have forgiveness and freedom from all your sins, truly can enable you to have unconditional love (without strings) towards your loved one.

I know the main reason I was able to show Victor love when he was out of control at times and wasn't acting lovable, was the simple fact that I knew that God loves me and has forgiven me for all the stuff I had done past, present and future. How can I not love him when I know I am so loved by my heavenly Father? He too, is able to love me when I'm not lovable because he has God's love inside of him and he knows how much he has been forgiven. It's hard to hold a grudge when you know that your own stuff is known and still forgiven! Remembering this fact brings tears to my eyes, as I know it is because God is holding us and keeping us together with His love through so many hard times. God is able to hold us even when we can't.

When Victor and I have gone through some of the most difficult times, I remind myself of these things:

1. We will get through this.
2. This will not last forever.
3. God hears us when we cry out to Him.
4. Our marriage was intended to last through good and bad times.
5. We need to remind each other how much we love each other.
6. Thank God that He promised to never leave us or forsake us.
7. Soon and very soon we are going to be in our forever home, Heaven!

To know that we will one day step into eternity and live in our forever home with our Heavenly Father makes life down here easier. We will go through hard times down here, but it's not the end of the story.

This Life Is Temporary

There was a time when I was so overwhelmed with so many things going on in my life that all I could do at that moment was cry. I cried and told Jesus I couldn't take it anymore; my heart couldn't continue to keep feeling overwhelmed. As I was literally on the floor crying I heard this in my heart: *"In my Father's house are many mansions: if it were not so, I would have told you. I go to prepare a place for you, and if I go and prepare a place for you, I will come back and take you to be with me that you also may be where I am."*

This was Jesus speaking right to my heart reminding me that this life is not going to be forever.
This brought such hope to my heart. The next day just to make sure I heard Him, I

was at a church service and saw this
scripture on a piece of paper on a chair
that I was sitting on! If you get overwhelmed
and feel like life gets more than you can
handle... Remember this scripture...

*"Do not let your hearts be troubled,
believe in God, believe also in Me. In my
Father's house are many mansions: if it
were not so, I would have told you. I go to
prepare a place for you, and if I go and
prepare a place for you, I will come back
and take you to be with me that you also
may be where I am."*
—John 14: 1-3

This is a truth you can hold on to.

Desperate for a Loved One?

For those of us who have been heartbroken over a loved one, I have some good news!

I remember being on my closet floor crying out of fear for my daughter and rehearsing all the "what if's" that could happen to my teenage daughter, who at the time was out partying and driving. The pain in my heart was more than I could handle. My thoughts kept going to "what if she gets in an accident and gets killed?" or "what if she hits someone and kills someone else? She will not only destroy their life, but she will spend the rest of her life in jail." What if…these "what if's" were killing me!

As I was once again on the floor out of complete desperation, I heard a scripture in my head. "Where can I go from Your Spirit? Or where can I flee from Your Presence?"

This I believe was God's Holy Spirit telling me that even though I cannot be there with my daughter to protect her from herself, and even try to prevent her from hurting herself, He was able to watch over her, He was able to keep her safe.

The moment I heard that, I agreed with Him. I said "you're right, I can't protect her and keep her from harm, but God, You can!" I got off the floor and left my closet with an incredible peace.

For those of you who have loved ones who are out there and are in situations that you know are dangerous, deadly or just completely upside down, put your loved one in that place...

Where can _____ go from Your Spirit?
Where can _____ go from Your Presence?

Trust them to God… He can do much more than you can.

A Most Beautiful Ending

I was standing putting dishes into the dishwasher when the thought that we had to go see my dad in California was so clear to me. I even got a song that my husband was to sing to him. At the same time, my husband was in a youth facility when he got the same impression with the same song!!

My dad had ALS and his health was declining rapidly and was in and out of the hospital. Within a few days, we were off to California with our baby boy, carry-on bags and guitar.

As we sat in his living room and caught up on life and played with our little one, Victor pulled out his guitar and told my dad that he wanted to sing a song and asked if he would mind. My dad said he would like that.

Victor started playing his guitar and singing this beautiful song about how much God loved my dad and how much He knew of the difficulties and challenges he was going through lately.

Tears started rolling down my dad's face as he listened to the song and absorbed the truth about the words being sung to him.

My dad shared with Victor that he had known Jesus as a little boy and even wanted to be a priest. He told him something happened to his faith when he went to Korea as a young man and found he and his platoon along with their chaplain being surrounded by the enemy. The chaplain that was supposed to be there for these young men ran to the jeep and drove away!

No wonder my dad had issues with his faith, how was a nineteen year old suppose to handle watching the " man of God" run away and act like a coward and leave these teen-agers to stay and fight like men? This brought things into focus for me as to why he struggled so much with his faith.

It's hard to put into words the joy I felt when I watched my husband pray with my dad to receive Jesus into his life... It was just 30 days later that my dad was able to see Jesus face to face.

I am so grateful that God hears our prayers and answers them, In His time. I had prayed for my dad for 18 years. I didn't have to witness my dad praying to receive Jesus. Just knowing that when he died he was going to go to heaven would have been enough.

I want to encourage those of you with love ones who have not yet put their faith in God, don't stop praying for them. Even if you have been praying for decades, keep praying! God hears your prayers and it's more of His heart and desire to have them with Him for eternity than ours!

If you would like more information or resources please visit:

VictorMarx.com
ATPMinistries.org

How precious also are Your thoughts to me,
O God!
How great is the sum of them!
If I should count them, they would be more
in number than the sand;
When I awake, I am still with You.

Psalm 139:17